"I have a weakness for beast fable, so the first part of *movingparts*, cunningly engaged with Aesop's 'The Fox and the Crow,' was a delight to me. Removing the moral, while keeping the story both ethically and existentially charged in a brisk series of prose poems brings this ancient material newly to life. Staying Greek, the latter two parts are engaged with the literary monument that is Sappho, and what she has meant, in particular, to English translators, especially Anne Carson, rather a monument herself. Sappho's notorious aporia provides Edward Carson with room to speculate both on how difficult it is to translate desire into language, and further, how the act of translation dually reifies and destabilizes a famous poet's work. His poems warily circle literary monoliths, and from time to time blow right through them, suddenly rendering their substance into breath."

Sarah Tolmie, author of *The Art of Dying*, *Trio*, and *Check*

"Edward Carson's *movingparts* is truly 'a temple of dapple in a tempest of cause.' His preoccupation with how our minds work – how they are sparked by desire and emotion – treats us to urgent explorations, like his meditation on Aesop's fable of the fox and the crow. Carson turns that encounter over and over in his hands to create a brilliant sixteen-faceted jewel, each surface polished by investigation, analysis and poetic wit. He then presents fourteen sonnets that are 'detonated' by lines from other poets, and that meld *desire memory anatomy*. And, finally, with exquisite control of his craft, Carson walks with Sappho through the terrain of the erotic, discussing 'the physics of craving.'"

Maureen Hynes, author of *Sotto Voce*

"Read each poem here aloud, they are riffs on myth and fable, they are koans, they are parables. Edward Carson's poems in *movingparts* move between what is or has been already said and what lies under the surface to be spoken. These poems are feminist. They are playful. His fox and crow poems, based on Aesop's fable, are jazzy riffs on wonder. The tight boxes of one section fall away to short lines and then to long-lined couplets, no punctuation so language is fluid as instinct and gesture."

Yvonne Blomer, author of *The Last Show on Earth*

THE HUGH MACLENNAN POETRY SERIES

Editors: Allan Hepburn and Carolyn Smart

Recent titles in the series

*moving*parts

EDWARD CARSON

McGill-Queen's University Press
Montreal & Kingston • London • Chicago

ISBN 978-0-2280-1666-3 (paper)
ISBN 978-0-2280-1749-3 (ePDF)
ISBN 978-0-2280-1750-9 (ePUB)

Legal deposit second quarter 2023
Bibliothèque nationale du Québec

Printed in Canada on acid-free paper that is 100% ancient forest free
(100% post-consumer recycled), processed chlorine free

We acknowledge the support of the Canada Council for the Arts.

Nous remercions le Conseil des arts du Canada de son soutien.

Library and Archives Canada Cataloguing in Publication

Title: Movingparts / Edward Carson.

Other titles: Moving parts

Names: Carson, Edward, 1948- author.

Series: Hugh MacLennan poetry series.

Description: Series statement: The Hugh MacLennan poetry
series | Poems.

Identifiers: Canadiana (print) 20220467293 | Canadiana (ebook)
20220467315 | ISBN 9780228016663 (paper) |
ISBN 9780228017509 (ePUB) | ISBN 9780228017493 (ePDF)

Classification: LCC PS8555.A7724 M68 2023 | DDC C811/.6—dc23

This book was typeset by Marquis Interscript in 9.5/13 Sabon.

for Lindsay and Matt

CONTENTS

MOVINGPARTS

mundus vult decipi, ergo decipiatur
the world wants to be deceived, so let it be deceived

CAVEAT

consider the canvas
coarse and
pronounced its

space a white linen
of clary sage oil

both medicinal
and spice

its plain weave
a reminder that

certain textures
as in a poem

literally pull
the paint

from the bristles
an admonition that

word for word
certain permutations

provisionally apply
where instructions
fail to appear

COUNTERPARTS

(fox & friend)

He told a lie. He wore it like a mask.
Paul Batchelor

During the sixth century BCE, Aesop, first mentioned
by Herodotus in *Histories*, was a celebrated Greek storyteller
and slave who won his freedom by telling fables that took
the form of social commentary and moral instruction.

THE FOX AND THE CROW

(IN WHICH BOTH OLD AND NEW APPEAR
TO BE UNRULY)

should parts of history rhyme and circle back the same
old same old is a pleasure worth repeating a backstory
and exordium of transmutation becoming a catalyst of
meaning where motive like metaphor matters within a
portrait of balance revealed and a familiar weaving of
continuity not so very different from the *fabula*
presented so a fox and crow are each a likeness of a
likeness made to crisscross centuries intersecting
storylines of a tale's common themes and creations a
poet each of allegorical though suspect beginnings being
both true and false proxies of capricious congregations

(IN WHICH FAST-MOVING MINDS ALL
AFLUTTER REASON TOGETHER)

in the minds of fox and crow an ever so intoxicating
brief belief is its own reward a virus of fact reordered
where voices are inspired to suppose true and false are
mere movements within a moment disconnected from
itself so fox and crow speed along with cause and
effect and a desire to continue believing yet still hope
for history to linger long enough to see that truth is a
fragment in a falling world and that what truly seduces
us are heartfelt feelings of intimacy and distance found
between an authenticity hastily assembled and moving
parts fashioned as a waking into counterfeit commotion

(IN WHICH THE TONGUE UNFURLS
IN A HURRIED SUCCESSION)

fox labours against the moon's pull lets fly a *pillaloo*
and half truth that remain a tug of war between virtue
and a vice a falsehood and a fact but fox is also a
sly solver of gravity's decree where the only temptation
is in keeping intention disguised while still plainly in
sight so haunted by crow wily fox inhabits the voice
of persuasion speaks from far below and yet comes out
on top while crow who lingers within the happy cajole
of coax and charm says much but suspects so very
little and the world wonders how it is that bad decisions
are probable if the chance of a good one is not possible

4

(IN WHICH STORIES ARE STARTLED
INTO LIFE LIKE DETONATIONS)

where expression is committed to filling a void a fox
unfettered let loose in the spring with something to say
now and again will huff and puff a lungful of air and
howl for a friend to be sung to and so overhear the
scribble scratch scrawl of a bird in a tree no twitter
that bird but a quarrel oozing song a bird whose hum
is a strident then gravelly sound from an off the cuff
caw to click rattle or coo its call a raucous formless
high pitched askew where clacking of bill is a rackety
note that asks whatever is fox thinking so uncertain
and free this disruption of space and bark of unease

(IN WHICH OPPOSITES ATTRACT
AND COUNTERPARTS QUARREL)

on and off with vim and hurl fox will voice a prismatic
harum scarum nugget of vowel consonant and croak its
spark and spit a pearl misunderstood by most a gasp
of high octane become a passing and defensive rasp
knowing when to be strategic and when to act so riddle
us riddle us crow in a tree the moon in its beak and
fox at its feet pray tell us true what is this chorus of
rudimentary speech what chthonic fable of toxic beat
and flow what air unspooled this riff of stuttering might
saying all the while this fox harangues a harrumph so
convincingly making singsong of praise into the night

(IN WHICH THE ARC OF THE TALE
EVOLVES THEN MOVES ON)

whereas fox is a loner with a self-assured sniff of the
hunt though relaxed with the facts crow is an idler
wide eyed and gullible and yet is a master of mimic
in airing a song but one has to ask what is it that fox
truly needs though in the difficult beauty of fox's mind
the singsong of crow sounds more like a cackle of
thrumming so better to question what one thinks is the
point for fox whose reason for being is the hustle of
the chase whereas crow going over things with a fine
tooth comb reveres the moonlight haunting fox's space
with a passion and belief in search of reveal and release

(IN WHICH ALL ASYMMETRICAL PARTS
ARE PARTLY UNKNOWN)

should black be accretion of trickle drip drop in a slow
cobalt wave of lilac blue gold then the darkness of
crow is a painting observed but seldom revealed where
the raucous concoctions in a misguided eye splash like
de Kooning or drizzle like Pollock this portrait of
feathers is a temple of dapple in a tempest of cause
at first reorganizing then redirecting its shape where
painterly crow so deficient in guile is more like a
moving iridescent shadow between all that's apparent
but rarely perceived like the feeling a hunter has in
the dark appearing from nowhere in search of the light

(IN WHICH THE PURSUIT BECOMES
A CONCEIT OF POSSIBILITY)

the known world is vast and changing the way crow
sees in spring the noxious leaves of the black walnut
are last to appear but first in autumn to tumble into
the wind and yet for fox all that is above and below
is simplified in the way moonlight simmers through
earth's blue green domain causing fox to shrug but
wonder if something's afoot knowing nothing of heaven
except the puzzling pleasure of solving an itch with a
scratch or rubbing against the trees where light breaks
itself apart like a mottle of memes the meaning for
which fox feels is more complex than meets the eye

(IN WHICH THINKING AND THOUGHTS
ARE NOT EVER TOGETHER)

crow thinks and as a consequence time and space will
stretch and compress calling forth the swoop up swivel
down of flight and imitating the feverish emotion the
frenetic feathering thought of crow's primordial mind a
reduction of thinking that takes time and the militance
of patience to know that fox speaks up every time
because fox is fox whereas crow holds back within the
overcast face of the moon waiting for the right moment
waiting as fox breathes in when crow breathes out and
fox barks as leaves quake and crow caws as light fades

(IN WHICH THE PERSISTENCE
OF DETECTION IS UNSUCCESSFUL)

it's pouring rain and nearly twelve in the congregation
of crow but crow is not in heaven yet though with an
attentive eye to midnight moon-licked fox preaches the
evangelical curve of right and wrong true and false is
by disposition a firebrand and storm eyed performer
weathering each downpour of belief and oh by the way
crow in a huddle or alight on a limb is obsessive and
grim where the fabrication and free for all at the
blustery edge of order are shaping what's trusted or
not questioning whether fox is part of a problem but
not at its heart asking for a clarity that never arrives

(IN WHICH THE HUBBUB OF VERB
IS A CLAMOUR AND BUZZ)

fox calls and crow replies and so it is how a chat with
fox is a river of invocation in eddies of acka woo and
ack awhoo cool as a cucumber fox says things that are
true and those that are not is aware of a time in a
great unraveling when crow caw raw caw rawed in the
night and yet fox's voice is a murmur of applause and
fabrication brimming with fact to dispel any doubts as
well as doubts to muddle a fact while crow from above
hungers for the many parts of a life it desires but not
the single one it needs listens to all that is said in the
way water poured in a vessel discovers a ready shape

(IN WHICH ONE THOUGHT MIDDLEMOST
SLIPS INTO ANOTHER)

other worldly crow haphazardly flying absently curves
when the wind curves the way a leaf flies in a breeze
the way an idea shapes the breath before even a sound
is made while fox in pursuing a different conversation
counts stars hunts for patterns knows numbers are even
or odd then promotes a quiet coercion made from a
wayward intention yet crow looking for attention is at
times euphoric inside the grasp of a talkative mind a
paradigm of migrating reason pursuing a purpose as
though within the slightest breeze a truthful word will
emerge only after a thought has escaped free as a bird

(IN WHICH PARTS OF A JOURNEY
ARE ODYSSEYS OF ABSOLUTE)

oh to be in the mind of fox is to wander through the
night and travel sleepless into the woods while always
eager to catch a whiff of any sniff there is in the air
but there's always a story of this earth to be told even
though it's barely a flicker of reality maybe more like
fragments of blood or jawbone of the dead gobbled
clean moreover the narrative and deceptions from fox
are what is spoken when half way between the whole
truth and a lie a fact and delusion its rhetoric of
expectation surely holds that fox is an angry pretence
of flummery a tongue lolling addiction to the hoodwink

(IN WHICH A PRESENCE IS LARGELY CONTINUOUS UNTIL IT'S NOT)

crow is who crow says crow is though not who crow
actually is in a real life but rather wishes to be so see
now noteworthy crow hunkered down with a low to
the earth pitch of caw hoooh caw wooo speak with a
momentary voice like a wind having no constant hiss
siphoned from the skittering slipstreams through the air
this fable being its song of change in a frayed acoustic
swooping voice more credibly precarious than it sounds
a mumblecore of hardscrabble exuberance captivated
spellbound rapt in moonlight it comes to a point in the
promise of crow a caesura in its call the perfect pause

(IN WHICH A VOICE OF BELIEF IS LEFT
TO ITS OWN DEVICES)

with crow the whole question of nourishment arises
then falls to fox so simple it seems like add and
subtract a way of seeing the story is not going to be
not what to believe from where crow is but on the
trail of what fox says yet being neither rhyme nor
reason true or false asking whether this is something
like a world of give and take and what might happen
next this undeniably must be fox as an instrument and
actor of trust within a skulk of metaphor in a pressing
temptation and tease that when made known hunts both
ways is neither perfectly aroused nor perfectly at ease

(IN WHICH MOMENTARY MOTION
IS EMBEDDED IN A BODY)

when fox explains things to crow meaning is slippery
often ruptured and tense a resistance of right or wrong
with the threat of never knowing what is meant but
surprise sometimes astonishment will muster itself like
a memory of moonlight and thought offering how a lie
heightens its truth with hints of both or where savvy
mobility in a lofty wind can be at least in fox's mind
reminders of both nearby and far as the crow flies and
yet fox dreams of the rituals of routine of hunting
down the hares or running past the hounds recognizing
the essence of pursuit entices what coaxes parts apart

PRIMARYPARTS

(desire memory anatomy)

We know how to say many false things like to real things, and we know, whenever we want to, how to utter true things.
Hesiod

all parts
seem to

be unruly
jockeying

for position
as thoughts

do while
words

blushing
assemble

constellations
in semantic

alignment
sentences

sinuously
metabolizing

between
what's meant

to mean and
what's not

so lovers
maneuvering

constellations
sinuously

converge
between

thoughts
while words

blushing
in phrases

appear to
be unruly

metabolizing
in

between a
configuration

of what is
semantic

and possibly
what's not

the tongue
unfurls in

a hurried
succession

of nibble
and knead

curl and
nudge where

the body
knows what

it truly
wants yet

the mind
wavers all

aflutter
thinking to

itself this
must be

a moment
of mind

over matter
a waggle

of wayward
thoughts

in a spree
of words

where words
are never

enough
what the

discerning
mind

reasons are
the physics

of love
oscillations

of flight
and the

intimacies
of acceleration

there is
always this

misgiving
this feeling

as if a
thought

is not quite
ready and

now and
again is not

quite real
its flow this

dalliance
of electrons

filling in
blank spaces

this mind
a breathlessly

fluid
coupling of

elementary
particles is

a life of
near misses

immaterial
in form yet

whatever its
reach it's un

selfconsciously
kaleidoscopic

as if as
soon as the

words are
startled into

life like
detonations

of thought
we begin to

realize what
is happening

opposites
attract and

counterparts
quarrel

having an
eye for it is

clearly but
not nearly

a proxy for
a sense of

what's false
yet finding

a half truth
digressing

astray is
of far more

use than
a useful lie

so as to
the quantum

of motion
and burdens

of time there
is room for

both doubt
and certainty

together with
the tyranny

of hint and
hunch that

modifies
the need we

seek to suit a
chosen want

something
as simple

as what we
know adds up

and all we
feel does not

entangled
in this in

between of
anticipation

and arrival
the mid

curve of
caress is

far more
hopeful than

persuasive
a deceit

of distance
and timing

both separate
and shared

but pausing
to rethink

again why
this arc of

our need
neither

advances
nor recedes

we're captured
in emotions

both moving
and fixed

when there's
too little

thought all
parts are

asymmetrical
and when

too much
the equation

regroups
commensurate

with new
parts unknown

a woman in
the portrait

appears to
pause much

as a viewer
also lingers

caught in
a glow of

afterlight
planning to

escape and
looking for

a way to
move on

slip clear
and out of

the frame
her face

breaks free
as the viewer

begins to
bend into

the canvas
much as she

too leans out
for a closer

look both
bound together

in a likeness
of thought

an acrobatic
angle and

conceit of
possibility

this careen
of peripheral

geometry
and force

of unbroken
reflection

what we're
hunting for

is not like
anything

we've heard
before

and so
resists our

metaphor
to the ear

unlikeness
of word

is clamour
and buzz a

chatter of
accumulation

rupture of
commotion

and lull its
brisk blare

of malice
and bite

of allure
is poetry

procured is
what the ear

overhears
as inside

we strain
to recognize

the hubbub
of verb the

racket of
noun in our

heads we
listen to

a *sub rosa*
of paradise

snared from
a wider silence

thinking and
thoughts are

never far
apart their

parts a
recipe of

harmony
and flow

or disarray
and sway

are anxious
unconformities

reciprocating
geologies of

longitudinal
size are

metaphors
of place

being both
close and

unreachable
while also

composite
proximities

but a
thought and

its words
can often be

a measure
of intimation

something like
a membrane

through which
the persistence

of detection
sifts all

that's more
or less

efficient on
its own terms

when Sappho
was young

and still
unknown and

yes singing
of love

her lover
took her

into her
mouth and

she shook in
the pleasure

of plum lips
and words yet

the moment
did not end

in a kiss
that became

a caress
but went on

and on her
embrace

a thought
that nothing

must be left
unsaid

like a voice
within a voice

saying what's
been forsaken

has likely just
gone missing

it's all too
far away says

Sappho as if
the world is

suddenly
inaccessible

so irresistibly
irretrievably so

she said let
me tell you

this story
when my

mind was
middlemost

between a
thought and

the raw
fragrance of

her touch
it was

uncommon
sense in

making sense
of a feeling

she said
now you

might ask
yourself

surely this
could lead

one astray
from one

encounter
to another

though there
should be

no reason
for it my

lover said
an instinct

like this is
less intention

than
flirtation

more
confession

than
sensation

A BODY HAS / TO BE A BODY

as one
thought

slips into
another

each word
sizeable

or small
one after

the other
is a body

of tectonic
mingle

a worldly
subduction

of parts in
a journey

of jigsaw
and guess

of syntax
and fidelity

the whole
thing's a

seismic
top down

bottom
up over

under
loop of

slide to
side the

convection
and plume

of narrative
in a lover's

words are
an odyssey

of absolute
a turmoil

of bodies
flesh to flesh

slippery
mutterings

dissolve
skid into

ecosytems
of rumour

and merge
through

our hand
held devices

it's a transient
experience

as a sense
of sincerity

and truth
breezes by

swiped at
high speed

squeezing
thought aside

yet Penelope
might have

found such
intrusions

convenient
each tap an

insatiable
touchstone

to historic
fabrications

of the self
and other a

selfie taking
time and

space apart
each minute

seeing cause
to pause a

provisional
recognition

BRUSHED WITH HIS THUMB THE NUT
OF HER NIPPLE

though it
seldom

takes time
to arrive

her desire
incremental

by design
speaks out

just lick it
she says

a refrain
of impatience

incidental
to his mind

in practice
instrumental

at all times
elemental

his want
a medley

of words
covertly

skimming
blindly

across the
surface of

belief
though

left to its
own

devices
the truth

of her
need is

bittersweet
desire

ceding to
a path of

least
resistance

though it
moves a

long way
on its own

a word is
momentary

motion
a sound

embedded
in a body

or poem an
orientation

largely
continuous

until it's
different

from what
we thought

so gender
too can be

a construct
and feeling

up against
another side

of thinking
saying

is there
a text in

this woman
a paratext

of words
clustering

dispersing
an index

of writing
referencing

within
personally

intersecting
points

*MISSING*PARTS

(decomposing Sappho)

*A fragment releases us from time and space, from rectilinear
complacency, from the noise of our own expectations into
a different dark lacuna, a stillness of study that is
possibly fathomless.*
Anne Carson

Herodotus relates the tale of a slave, Rhodōpis, a beautiful and
highly educated courtesan, artist, and raconteur who was reputed
to be a companion and secret lover of Aesop. Her freedom was
eventually purchased at Naucratis in Egypt by a wealthy
merchant, Charaxus, older brother of the lyric poet Sappho.

prepare the agile mind for the truth not

the truth for the mind for the truth can
be in the moment tempting and blinding

by itself unthinking or even fleeting the

way turn off today is tomorrow's attract
or yes even reason like metaphor hiding

in plain sight means more than it is yet

she says not for the first time this truth

is desire for which there's beauty but no
past tense a flowering stitchwork shaped

in the present in no time at all initiating

a feeling of returning affection and lure
this itinerant petition foretelling a history

of surrender and resistance lurking there

IF EVER BEFORE / YOU CAUGHT MY VOICE
FAR OFF

in time the one loved becomes the lover

desire will go where it can't help but go
a convoluted need jostling for something

untethered reversing what might be how

easily a feeling thought to be unthinkable
becomes a thought and so will turn into

what is unaccounted for a love having no

thought of being taken into account where

wily words are prudently dismantled and
careful parts assembled in a voice within

a voice and yet such solace is a fleeting

failing comfort taking the place of another
where love knows desire is its nature as

if what is returned is not part of a whole

murmuration mutters in the air chatters

coos and rattles its unruly language as
flight of lopsided consonance repeating

the one and rearranging the many is on

the whole an apostrophe of sorts of self
and other something you say is let loose

in a lover composed in a give and take

erotic exchange where a question always

embraces its answer and voices scurrying
into each reply are personalities shaping

a blush of clarity with a necessary truth

and so you seduce with a dizzying kiss
these bodies cascading crowded with desire

uncertain which way to turn or look next

QUICK SPARROWS OVER
THE BLACK EARTH

she touches us or we touch her she who

in her words is who she is never at all
who you'd expect the same then as now

her writings darting like sparrows urgent

in flight airborne and midair where the
wind goes missing her every word saying

life is shade shadow silhouette a light or

dark before this long ago time then later

her missing words deep in the terrain of
a page like ghosts haunting us with their

shameless surprise the small hooked stories

arriving nearby or newly freed carefully
dispersing into a consciousness impossible

to miss more than dangerous to overlook

IF SHE DOES NOT LOVE, SOON
SHE WILL LOVE

dual and reciprocal yet incoming more

than realized her love is missing from
the thought of it and also by extension

its plain unpredictability fails to appear

but there is promise of a true substance
and balance in the swale of bare thigh

and breasts the coveted furrows of sex

and textures of pleasure that combine in

a desire notoriously subjective so wisely
calibrated and conceived that you might

truly say well yes actually that is what

was anticipated all along from the nude
descending a staircase dividing her body

in fragments both a fallacy and a truth

when speaking words similar to a truth

that concentrate the mind or congregate
into a lover's artifice of lure a flutter

of parts this way or that brings together

a narrative so credible even the autumn
leaves still believe in their branches and

nested thoughts assembled by degree or

pulling sense together are believed to be

of sound sincerity as if every word were
true and yet the idea is for words to stir

like truth and truths to be not hidden or

forgotten where authenticity and purpose
run capriciously and veracity in loving is

honesty in flux moving straight or curved

WHOEVER HE IS WHO OPPOSITE YOU / SITS AND LISTENS

within her mind love nimbly evolves to

something at the crossover of this starry
light and dark this nightfall of narrative

is true and false is not unlike the binary

her mind makes a shape of shared truth
and similarity where all thought will lead

to an idea then to a theory then to a test

of what if what is what was what will be

so truth means her love has been considered
a body resisting inside its own obsolescence

a sex uncommon or commonplace engaging

some other overwhelming truth offering us
safe harbour neither better nor worse than

what's not to be believed until it happens

this mischief of desire is under our skin

in every way a presence we can't hold
for long a trick of the body saying stay

here awhile where resistance is futile but

pleasure is in the end a likeness talking
beneath the radar of allure its muscular

draw a cautionary tale and cipher difficult

to crack easy to delight in which there is

the sweet persuasion of nuance intimately
passing through the ever conscious mind

the enigma of this exterior reflecting this

interior of sense is first merely a murmur
and then leisurely a pulse within our lips

her back arching into this tongue's caress

this might be high or low where Sappho

plays though hearing her could make it
so saying her words in every measure is

a nuzzle of saxophone a fondle of guitar

a music of up all night and swinging till
dawn so in the empty spaces where her

musing is not there there isn't anything

to see yet aware we are of widespread

sounds oozing from her headless lines all
intervals of premonition saying look here

look back a while with a wonder where

the tempo rises to a fall resolving up and
down as the piano teasing out a solo says

let's see more where nothing seems to be

at every part rose lips touch and tongue

leads to too much pleasure her swelling
quench and grooves curving ripe in this

steady pitch at every pleat and fold and

yet in call and response we can devise
allocate elaborate details leaning into

this desire with fevered syncopation but

also dislocations of positions with no

end in mind other than to prolong this
pleasing play enticing out particulars of

difference realized in this world of our

loving the press dip flit and pulse of
our bodies a dismantling of minutiae

shaking us at every stroke and speed

MY / MIND LIKE A MOUNTAIN
WIND FALLING

if truth be told desire assumes escalation

a variable gust in the open trees of all
arousal and temptation a knotty strength

deep in dance and drift where nothing's

fixed for too long though the mind will
sometimes flail in the sharp open ended

physics of craving its rush and swirl giving

way to where a feeling reassembles itself

anew so you might think to ask yourself
if this attraction is a wind and are we

slowly falling closer to each other where

physics pulling us together also opens up
a singularity and concurrence only to find

all things are likely rarely inconceivable

as the entrance to another mind a refrain

cut into pieces of words will chase then
alternate transform and reveal a roaming

explanation of minor thoughts into bits

keeping track of thinking in other parts
where knowing what is in the mind of

the other is a question of how you feel

whereas the other trusts that love arrives

when and where it can not always true
to itself though more like a shadow on

a wall always in motion always offering

some other self to be uncovered sure to
exist both inside and out a methodology

of what we do not who we say we are

a woman wavers and slews in search of

her words that reach out or veer to tempt
then drift or quarrel until swallowed into

the whiter noise of the emptied page her

voice a sonant sibilant of hiss or buzz a
syllable reluctantly unmoored prismatically

attentive to pressing gently forward a sing

and song of a sound we're moved to ask

could this be a calling of chant or psalm
or maybe even a collage of consciousness

nimbly breathing out each breath breathed

in leaving behind a sceptical mind and a
vast emptiness as a starting point to fill in

each poem setting free all that is missing

second by second we listen to a rise and

fall of a voice its oscillations in a bluesy
jazz of unearthly sounds outflowing like

birds in flight from low to high the curl

of each note stretched and skipping into
another and we whose lives have chased

countless twists and turns lean into this

with a spirited thought and voice of true

investigation living within a melody's path
its journey winding forward teeming with

bend or loop veering at times to vexed

complaint in a mind whose lyrics sleuth
in wary diversion or wise restraint where

words can lie and others speak the truth

a poem strays with occasional change to

the vanishing points of intersecting lives
so desire roams within a whim as will

each lover tilting horizontal or vertical

the mind in its thinking adding steps to
how what is true revises and renews yet

a poem is cheerfully woven in peripatetic

ways or startling in the way of having to

catch your breath each time belief betrays
so a desire will stray and is meddlesome

likewise serpentine saying there are false

things in the world that need to be seen
to be true while there are others needing

to be true before they can truly be seen

it takes ages before knowing why not much

lasts for long or that our expression of love
vanishing over years and distance refashions

itself in a smoulder and language of desire

this condensed drama we inhabit is unsettled
looking back tangentially to something more

each line is a nervous apparition a moving

trace and triggered energy in welcoming

words that seem to be states of suspension
in defiance of illumination at its hard core

and frame the poem bends stretching space

and questions the moment's widening face
this ghost gathering time provoking pause

swells in memory sting and chain reaction

the mind learns to humour this distance

between what is there and what is not
that what remains unspoken might also

be unsayable in the way a mind coming

into its own is seldom certain of merely
one thing or longs to know what it is it

wants to say so yes we know this much

is true in something like love your voice

will often skip by some troublesome truth
leaving the sound of its absence escaping

to where your voice meets a silence like

no other an open space open to knowing
its motive for being a defensive carapace

of the mind going on about its business

oh to the pleasure in a desire that flows

where you flow or flexes when you flex
this curling of toes and camber of breast

follow your every prompt and nudge and

curb the curve of your bristling give and
take where nothing lives in a straight line

yet sometimes this fire along the spine is

the mind flensing itself adjusting a voice

more singular than shared its close up not
this preening of you and I but one where

speaking its mind is a flight from flirtation

a bracing beeline as the crow flies to itself
darting along a thread of deceit or honesty

it jostles and strays ruthlessly wholehearted

NEITHER FOR ME HONEY NOR
THE HONEY BEE

where a bee burrows deeply in a bloom

a love has room for being without truth
whereas a lie artfully swarms in and out

having no room to spare its imitation of

truth doing the labour of the lie its hive
harder to inhabit harder still to relinquish

this sting of language this fragrant honey

maddened flight now here now there now

being neither concealed nor far from mind
turning back to history's ways in countless

loves yet both welcoming and withholding

the bees approach with artifice and wing
the threshold of far horizons their arrival

flush in prophesy and honeycomb of doubt

is it possible Sappho's missing words are

merely transparent the appearance of each
looked through and no longer apparent or

possibly they are simply diminishing with

age as we all must do some plainly have
not survived the years which may be the

truth of things but maybe the airy spaces

are shrewd and migratory thoughts on an

absence that seems a little sly even double
edged in its need to perplex and conceal

like desire itself an unlikely perseveration

with its very nature about the provocation
of errant words evading our every touch

now extinct having lost the ability to fly

TO GUARD AGAINST A VAINLY
BARKING TONGUE

there is in heaven a bricolage of sounds

at night the auroras hiss above the earth
and barking crow in circles flies replying

with windswept words while history drifts

off course inside a topsy-turvy ion sky
sizzling like voices trying to fashion new

tales of duplicity or lie its undulations like

a wave finding equilibrium between groove

and crest a path of contrary meaning seen
in the balancing of time and its symmetry

so listen listen listen when you can and

heed the wind's advice its plangent voice a
motion always on the threshold of breaking

out like life tumbling clear a motley truth

YOU WILL GO YOUR WAY AMONG
DIM SHAPES

there is much to consider like where you

long to go depends on where you already
are as when desire has become a cloud

between us or how a mind can absently

linger then retreat from the thick of some
misgiving a doubting and undoing of a lie

in all its enticements or discontents so this

unease between us is an enigmatic intimacy

leaving us at the brink of the long division
of pleasure a prickliness and breathlessness

already tasted but not consumed learned but

not acted upon the hither and thither of its
coming and going a centre stage sensibility

impossible to say where it's going to or why

with everything moving and much to say

out of nowhere something catches the eye
then disappears never really there or there

for a time before this moment moves on

Sappho says the truth of seeing can also
be what's not there but in the mind's eye

it's the raw geometry of what we'll make

of never quite knowing how to bring back

what has long escaped or in thinking how
what in the middle of moving comes to a

standstill this presence at the very edge of

surprise of the unseen a mystery of time
this intention to which the mind holds us

this pulse within a predetermined motion

NOTES AND ACKNOWLEDGMENTS

Thanks to my editor Allan Hepburn as well as Carolyn Smart for their readings, encouragement, and continued support; and, as always, to Brian Henderson – "comrades in words since 1965" – who never fails to answer the mail.

caveat: with a nod to Fiona Benson

He told a lie. He wore it like a mask: from Paul Batchelor, "The Well," *London Review of Books* 43, no. 22 (18 November 2021): 32.

We know how to say . . . from Hesiod, *Theogony*, "Invocation to the Muses," l. 28–9.

the form of a motion: from A. R. Ammons, *Sphere: The Form of a Motion* (New York: W.W. Norton & Company, 1995).

my tongue flies away: from Doireann Ní Ghríofa, "First Date on Azul Street," *Lies* (Dublin: Dedalus Press, 2018), 9.

in our every cell / a tiny alphabet: from Maureen N. McLane, "were fragments enough . . . ," *Same Life* (New York: Farrar, Straus and Giroux, 2008), 3.

with my eyes / shut: from Ciaran Carson, "I Ask Myself,"
On the Night Watch (Winston-Salem: Wake Forest
University Press, 2010), 27.

he slides his hand up her leg: from Anne Carson, *The
Beauty of the Husband: A Fictional Essay in 29 Tangos*
(New York: Vintage Books, 2002), 15.

faces / grinning from the dark: from John Burnside,
"An Essay in *Sangfroid*," *Still Life with Feeding Snake*
(London: Cape Poetry, 2017), 54.

paradise caught in the ear: from Maureen N. McLane,
"unmeasured the white . . . ," *Same Life* (New York:
Farrar, Straus and Groux, 2008), 5.

the mind in the act: from Wallace Stevens, "Of Modern
Poetry," *The Collected Poems of Wallace Stevens*
(New York: Alfred A. Knopf, 1972), 239.

the bit of seedcake out of my mouth: from James Joyce,
Ulysses (New York: Vintage International, 1990),
Section 18, 782.

how my lover's skin smelt of it: from Fiona Benson,
"Androgeus," *Times Literary Supplement*,
2 October 2020.

a body has / to be a body: from Ulalume Gonzalez de
León, "In Search of the Lost Body," *Poetry Daily /
Exchanges*, Spring 2021, trans. Terry Ehret, John Johnson,
Nancy J. Morales (Iowa City).

a sweet hand right now: from Maureen N. McLane, "Mz N Enough," *Mz N: the serial* (New York: Farrar, Straus and Giroux, 2016), 53.

brushed with his thumb the nut of her nipple: from Simon Armitage, "To His Lost Lover," *Book of Matches* (London: Faber and Faber, 1993).

is there a woman in this text: from Mary Jacobus, "Is There a Woman in This Text," *New Literary History* 14, no. 1, Problems of Literary Theory (Autumn 1982): 117–41.

A fragment releases us . . . from Anne Carson, "Stillness," Public Lecture, Isabel Bader Theatre, The Centre for Comparative Literature, University of Toronto, 4 February 2020, 18:29–18:45.

Aphrodite of the spangled mind: all titles in *missing*parts from *If Not, Winter: Fragments of Sappho*, trans. Anne Carson (New York: Vintage Books, 2003), 3.

if ever before / you caught my voice far off: (Sappho/Carson 3)

fine birds brought you: (Sappho/Carson 3)

quick sparrows over the black earth: (Sappho/Carson 3)

if she does not love, soon she will love: (Sappho/Carson 5)

to tell / tongue / to tell tales: (Sappho/Carson 33)

whoever he is who opposite you / sits and listens: (Sappho/Carson 63)

close / to your sweet speaking: (Sappho/Carson 63)

no speaking / is left in me: (Sappho/Carson 63)

you burn me: (Sappho/Carson 77)

my / mind like a mountain wind falling: (Sappho/Carson 99)

two states of mind in me: (Sappho/Carson 107)

having been breathed out: (Sappho/Carson 115)

clearsounding: (Sappho/Carson 143)

sweetworded desires: (Sappho/Carson 147)

Sappho, why: (Sappho/Carson 271)

you would let loose your longing: (Sappho/Carson 187)

she bites her tender mind: (Sappho/Carson 191)

neither for me honey nor the honey bee: (Sappho/Carson 295)

transparent dress: (Sappho/Carson 349)

to guard against a vainly barking tongue: (Sappho/Carson 319)

you will go your way among dim shapes: (Sappho/
Carson 115)

my thinking / not thus / is arranged: (Sappho/Carson 9)